Badminton

Clive Gifford

SEA-TO-SEA

Mankato Collingwood London

This edition first published in 2010 by
Sea-to-Sea Publications
Distributed by Black Rabbit Books
P.O. Box 3263, Mankato, Minnesota
56002

Copyright © Sea-to-Sea Publications
2010

Printed in USA

Library of Congress Cataloging-in-Publication Data

Gifford, Clive.
  Badminton / Clive Gifford.
      p. cm. -- (Know your sport)
  Includes index.
  ISBN 978-1-59771-215-6 (hardcover)
  1. Badminton--Juvenile literature. I. Title.
  GV1007.G54 2010
  796.345--dc22
                                        2008045011

9 8 7 6 5 4 3 2

Published by arrangement with the Watts
Publishing Group Ltd., London

Series editor: Jeremy Smith
Art director: Jonathan Hair
Series designed and created for
Franklin Watts by Painted Fish Ltd.
Designer: Rita Storey
Editor: Nicola Edwards
Photography: Tudor Photography,
    Banbury

Note: At the time of going to press, the statistics
and player profiles in this book were up to date.
However, due to some players' active participation
in the sport, it is possible that some of these may
now be out of date.

Picture credits
Glyn Kirk/Action Plus pp 6, 9, 19, 21 and
25; Neil Tingle/Action Plus pp 7 and 27.

Cover images: Tudor Photography,
Banbury.

All photos posed by models.
Thanks to Naushad Chaudhry, Lindsey
Cruse, Polly Galis, Victoria Harrison, and
Jack Morris.

The Publisher would like to thank Blessed
George Napier Catholic School for the use
of their sport facilities and coach, Katie
Shires, for her assistance.

Taking part in a sport is a
fun way to get in shape, but
like any form of physical
exercise it has an element of
risk, particularly if you are unfit,
overweight, or suffer from any
medical conditions. It is advisable
to consult a healthcare
professional before beginning
any program of exercise.

Contents

What is Badminton?

Badminton can be fun to play in your own backyard. However, when it is played at a competitive level, it is a fast, explosive sport where one or two players per side use a racket to hit a shuttlecock back and forth over a net. It is one of the most popular sports in the world. The top international players are phenomenal athletes, able to hit the shuttle at speeds of more than 185mph (300km/h).

The Aim of the Game

Badminton is played as singles, doubles, and mixed doubles—one man and one woman per side. In a game of badminton, the aim is to score points by hitting a shot that your opponent cannot reach or by forcing them into making an error. The shuttlecock must not touch the floor of the court, land outside the court, or land in the net. Only one contact with the racket is allowed per side before the shuttlecock travels over the net to the opposition.

The Scoring System

A badminton match is usually the best of three or five games. Until recently, each game was played until one side scored 15 points, with points only being won by the player serving (or pair serving, in a doubles match). In 2006, a new scoring system was adopted. Points are now won by either side, not just the server. Games are won by the first player to reach 21 points, but if the score reaches 20–20, then the game continues until either one player gets two points clear (i.e. 25–23) or one player reaches 30 (i.e. 30–29).

Denmark's Kenneth Jonassen dives at full stretch to retrieve the shuttle during a crucial match at the 2006 All England Open Badminton Championships.

Chinese star player, Jun Zhang, leaps high into the air to hit an overhead smash shot. Top players are superb athletes able to cover the court with ease and react rapidly.

The History of Badminton

Games played with a form of shuttlecock and some sort of bat or racket existed centuries ago in Ancient Greece, China, and India. In the 1860s, a version of the game, called Poona, was played by British soldiers stationed in India. Badminton gets its name from the home of the Duke of Beaufort, where a version of the game was first played in 1873. Within a few years, rules were drawn up and clubs were formed. The first major championships, the All-England Championships, began in 1899. In 1934, nine member nations (Canada, Denmark, England, France, Ireland, Netherlands, New Zealand, Scotland, and Wales formed the International Badminton Federation (IBF), now called the Badminton World Federation (BWF).

A Global Sport

The International Badminton Federation (IBF) organized its first major championship, the Thomas Cup, for national men's teams in 1948. A similar women's event, the Uber Cup, followed in 1957, and the World Championships first took place in 1977. Badminton reached the Olympics as a demonstration sport in 1972 and achieved full medal sport status at the 1992 Barcelona Olympics.

Badminton has been a popular part of every Commonwealth Games since 1966. Today, from small beginnings, the IBF has 151 member nations and in 2006 changed its name to the Badminton World Federation (BWF).

Three Winners

Despite being held regularly since 1948, the Thomas Cup has only ever been won by three nations—Indonesia, Malaysia, and China.

Badminton for All

One of the most appealing aspects of the sport is that it can be played by people of all ages and abilities. You do not have to be incredibly tall or powerful. Badminton is one of the few sports where women and girls can compete directly with men and boys. Mixed doubles with one man and one woman per side is one of the most enjoyed versions of the game. At the higher levels of the game, players do have to be athletic and highly skillful.

Training and Preparation

Badminton is a high-energy, athletic sport that tests all parts of your body. Players lunge, dive, and stretch in all directions during a game. It may seem really boring warming up and stretching your muscles, but it can help prevent injuries and give you the advantage over an opponent.

Warming Up and Down

Allow around 15 minutes for preparation before a game. Start with warming up by walking fast, jogging, and running a few short sprints. Some players like to practice jumping and swinging their arms briskly. Warming up gets the blood pumping around your body and your muscles ready for the activity ahead. Warming down after training or a match is also important. This can be less vigorous and involves light jogging, walking, and some gentle stretches.

Stretch for Success

After warming up, stretch your key muscles, which include all your major leg muscles—the hamstrings, groin, quadriceps (thigh muscles), and calves, as well as your lower back, shoulders, and arms. Stretches should always be gentle and the stretch held for a few seconds before being repeated. Take stretching seriously and ask your coach to suggest a full range of stretches. Try to have a few minutes on court before a match to practice some shots gently, which will help you to get a feel for the court.

Stretching

With the soles of both feet flat on the floor, this player stretches his groin muscles.

This player holds her upper arm with her other hand to stretch part of her shoulder.

Keeping his pelvis and toes on the floor, this player arches his back to stretch the muscles.

8

Sidestep

This player sidesteps across the court while keeping his eyes on the shuttlecock. From a ready position, he slides one foot over so that it is beside the other foot. As this occurs, he slides or hops his other foot across and repeats the movement.

Gail Emms and Nathan Robertson

Dates of birth: July 23, 1977 (Emms)
May 30, 1977 (Robertson)

Nationality: British

Height: 5ft 3in (1.62m) / 6ft 2in (1.88m)

Weight: 61kg (134lb) / 183lb (83kg)

Achievements (all Mixed Doubles)
2006 World Championship winners
2006 Commonwealth Games gold medal
2004 Olympic silver medal
2004 European Championship gold medal
2002 Commonwealth Games team gold medal

2006 Madrid silver medal

Both Gail Emms and Nathan Robertson took up badminton at a young age. They first played together at age 15 but it wasn't until 2001 that they paired up as adults and won their first title, the Dutch Open. Working brilliantly well together, the pair have won many mixed doubles titles and in 2006, were world ranked number one.

Running a Mile

Badminton is a highly athletic sport that can be played by people of all ages. In a typical three-game match, a player runs approximately 1.5 miles (2.4km).

Fitness and Footwork

Away from playing matches, badminton players work hard on staying in shape, and being sharp and able to perform at their peak for long periods. Players practice moving rapidly around the court, using smooth, quick footwork and stepping moves, such as the shuffle step and the sidestep.

Emms and Robertson in action close to the net.

Court and Equipment

Competitive badminton is played with rackets and shuttlecocks indoors on a wooden court measuring 44ft (13.4m) long and 17ft (5.18m) wide for singles. For doubles, it increases in width by 18in (.46m) on either side of the court.

Points and Faults

Serving starts each point and has its own strict rules (see pages 14 to 15). Once a rally has begun, a player scores a point if his or her shot travels over the net and lands in the court of the opponent. If the shuttle lands on the line, then it is considered "in." Players also score points if their opponent fails to hit the shuttle back over the net and

into their court. When one player commits a fault, a point is awarded to their opponent. It is a fault if the shuttle hits the player's body or clothing, or if the player hits the shuttle so that it touches the ceiling. It is also a fault if a player touches the net with his or her racket, body, or clothing, or if the shuttle is caught on the racket head and then thrown across the net.

Shuttlecocks and Rackets

Shuttlecocks or shuttles come in two basic types—plastic and feathered. The plastic type lasts longer and costs less and is the type you are most likely to start with. The feathered type is used in competitions. Feathered shuttlecocks are very delicate and are made up of 16 goose feathers set into a cork base.

The Court

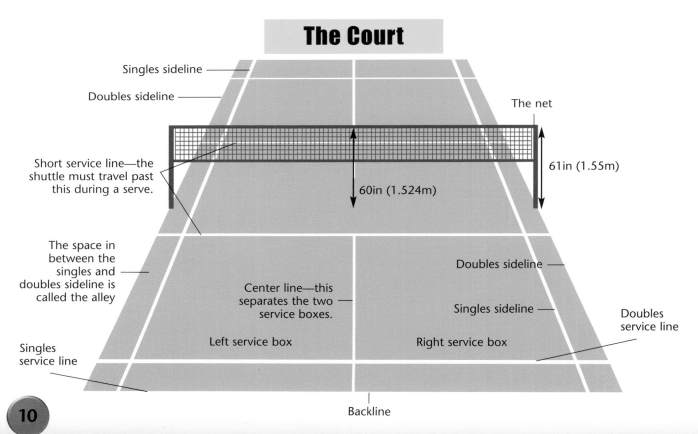

Singles sideline

Doubles sideline

The net

Short service line—the shuttle must travel past this during a serve.

61in (1.55m)

60in (1.524m)

The space in between the singles and doubles sideline is called the alley

Doubles sideline

Center line—this separates the two service boxes.

Singles sideline

Doubles service line

Left service box

Right service box

Singles service line

Backline

This player is about to make a shot with the shuttlecock falling close to the sideline. Judging whether an opponent's shot is going to land in or out is an important part of the game.

Clothing

When you start out, you need little special clothing to play the game. What you wear, though, should be loose-fitting and made of cotton to absorb sweat. A comfortable t-shirt, shorts, and thick cotton socks are ideal. If you join a badminton club and play in competitions, you may be asked to wear mostly white clothing. Many players wear sweatbands on their wrists. Whether you do or not, carry a towel to dry your hands, face, and racket grip. Also carry a bottle of water to take sips from between games.

Modern badminton rackets are light, sometimes weighing less than 3.5oz (100g), so they can be swung rapidly and easily. The racket head is separated from the handle grip by a long, narrow shaft. Most modern rackets are made of composite materials like graphite. Rackets come in different weights and grip sizes. Your racket is the one piece of specialist equipment you need to buy, so choose it carefully. Ask an experienced player or a badminton coach to recommend a suitable racket for your age and ability level.

Footwear

Indoor court shoes suitable for badminton should be worn. These should have plenty of cushioning inside to protect your feet, should feel comfortable and have a light-colored sole that will not mark the court. Good badminton shoes should last you a long time, especially if you only wear them on court and use different shoes to walk to and from the gym.

A loose-fitting t-shirt won't restrict your movements.

A sweatshirt is useful to keep you warm before and after a game. It is also essential to drink water between games.

Thick cotton socks help prevent your feet from getting blisters.

Good court shoes provide grip and support your feet.

11

Grip and Hit

Some badminton shots require a lot of power. Others demand a gentle touch. All, though, require rapid reactions and fast movement from the player, both in moving into a good position to play the shot and in choosing the correct grip for the shot to be played.

Test Your Grip

The forehand is the most frequently used grip in badminton. It is used for shots on the forehand side of your body and those around your head. To test whether you have a good forehand grip, you should be able to place the racket face flat against a wall. During a game you will have to change between forehand and backhand grips. Use your free hand to turn the shaft of the racket to switch between grips.

The Forehand and Backhand Grips

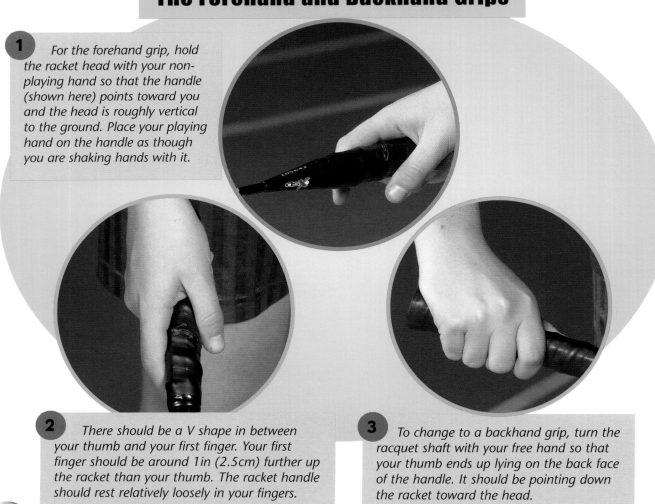

1 For the forehand grip, hold the racket head with your non-playing hand so that the handle (shown here) points toward you and the head is roughly vertical to the ground. Place your playing hand on the handle as though you are shaking hands with it.

2 There should be a V shape in between your thumb and your first finger. Your first finger should be around 1in (2.5cm) further up the racket than your thumb. The racket handle should rest relatively loosely in your fingers.

3 To change to a backhand grip, turn the racquet shaft with your free hand so that your thumb ends up lying on the back face of the handle. It should be pointing down the racket toward the head.

The Tap

The Push

The Whip

Here are the three movement actions used in badminton shots—the tap, the push, and the whip action.

The Ready Position

The ready position is the stance you take in general after hitting a shot. You should be alert and in a position to move in any direction. Keep your knees slightly flexed and your feet around shoulder-width apart. If you're a right-handed player, place your left foot half a step ahead of your right. It is important to stay on the balls of your feet so that you are springy and bouncy.

Basic Shot Movements

Nearly all badminton shots involve one of three types of movement of the racket—a tap, a push, or a whip. The tap is where you cock (bend back) your wrist and then spring it forward to meet the shuttle. The shuttle should travel away at a good speed and you should feel a gentle rebound like hitting a nail with a hammer. The push is a more gentle action, where you bend back your

wrist and keep it bent back as you push through the shuttle. This sends the shuttle away at a slower speed. The whip is a powerful action that generates maximum force and shuttle speed. The hand is cocked at the wrist and the arm swings quickly through. As the racket makes contact with the shuttle, the wrist uncocks, generating extra power. The arm follows through.

Practice Makes Perfect

As a complete beginner, it is a good idea to practice hitting the shuttle away from a court. Use the different shot actions to hit the shuttle, and work on moving around the court to get into a good position. You can practice on your own or with a friend. Ask your teacher or coach to suggest some fun games and exercises to combine moving around the court with getting a feel for hitting the shuttle.

Serving

At the beginning of a game of badminton, a coin is tossed to decide who goes to which end ends and who serves first from the right-hand service box. The serve must be played with the server standing inside their service box with both feet on the ground. They serve toward the service box diagonally opposite.

Service Rules

The server must hit the shuttle so that it lands inside the service box containing the receiver. At the point the racket hits the shuttle, the racket head must be pointing downward or below a level position. The shuttle must be hit below waist-height and the racket must connect with the shuttle's base first. If any of the above rules are broken, the receiver gains a point and serves. If the server wins the point, they serve again from the other service box.

The Serve

Front foot points toward target. Shuttle held lightly between fingers and thumb.

Server's eyes stay on the shuttle. Racket arm swings through.

1 With feet shoulder-width apart, one behind the other, hold the shuttle at arm's length in front of you and slightly to your racket side. The racket, held in a forehand grip, is taken back with a cocked wrist. As you drop the shuttle, swing your racket forward using an underarm movement. Twist your body from a side-on to a front-on position.

2 Move your body weight so that it is over your front foot. Uncock your wrist as your racket connects with the shuttle. The racket drives through the shuttle sending it forward and upward. The racket swing continues after impact so that it follows through high.

The Backhand Low Serve

Wrist cocked.
Shuttle held gently.

Eyes follow the shuttle's path.

1 *Stand balanced with one foot to the side and behind your front foot. Hold the shuttle with a straight arm well away from your body. The elbow of your racket hand should be kept high. Ideally, the only part of your body that moves during this serve is your racket arm. Start by taking the racket back by bending your elbow.*

2 *Bring the racket forward using the push action (see p13), keeping your wrist cocked. Let go of the shuttle just before you make contact, making sure you hit the shuttle base and at a height below your waist. The aim with this shot is to send it low over the net and let it drop in the front of the receiver's service court.*

Low Serves

Low serves can be hit on the backhand or forehand side. They aim to land just in the front of the receiver's service court. This forces the receiver to net their return or to lob it up weakly so that the server can hit a winning shot. You can use low and high serves to vary how you start a point. A high serve sends the shuttle over the receiver to the back of the court.

The flick serve is a high serve that looks like a low serve to the front of the court but instead travels over the receiver and toward the back of the court. The extra power needed is achieved by tightening the grip and flicking the wrist quickly and powerfully just before impact.

Making Shots

Once a rally is under way, players try to force their opponents to move around the court, and watch carefully for an opening to attack. Winning shots can rely on power, but often they depend on making the right choice of shot, playing it with skill, and placing it well.

Attack or Defend?

As you play a rally, you have to make many decisions. Your first thought should be to try to attack, playing the shuttle whenever possible above net height, so that you can hit downward. In many situations, though, such a shot is not possible, and you will have to play a more defensive shot. Just as

important is to match the right shot to the shuttle and your position. Trying to play an overhead smash when the shuttle is too low, for example, will often end with the shuttle in the net. In that situation, a drive shot (see pages 20–21) may be the better choice.

Different Shots

The different badminton shots can be divided up into shots that are played on the backhand side, the forehand side, or, when directly above you, around the head. They can also be grouped into shots hit overhead, to the side, or underarm. Mastering a large number of the many shots available in badminton takes a lot of practice, but the more shots you can play confidently the more tools you will have with which to beat your opponents.

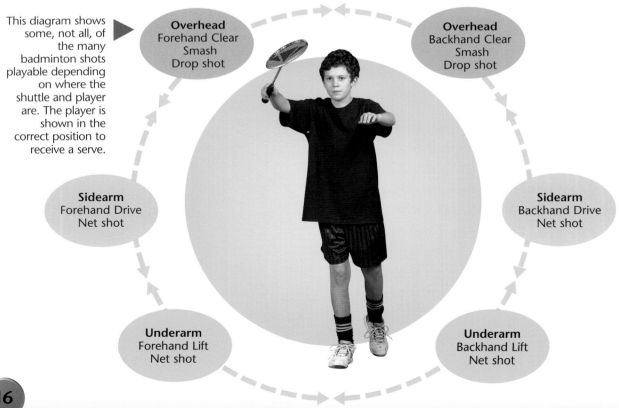

This diagram shows some, not all, of the many badminton shots playable depending on where the shuttle and player are. The player is shown in the correct position to receive a serve.

Overhead
Forehand Clear
Smash
Drop shot

Overhead
Backhand Clear
Smash
Drop shot

Sidearm
Forehand Drive
Net shot

Sidearm
Backhand Drive
Net shot

Underarm
Forehand Lift
Net shot

Underarm
Backhand Lift
Net shot

The Underarm Lift

1 *Using a forehand grip, the player gets her weight over her front foot. She lunges forward and, using a tapping or whipping action, swings her racket underarm.*

2 *The player aims to make contact with the shuttle well in front of her, hitting it upward and forward over the net and into the rear of her opponent's court.*

Underarm Lifts

Also known as underarm clears or lobs, the underarm lift sends the shuttle high to the back of the court. It is a good shot to use when you're close to the net and the shuttle is too low for you to attack. If your opponent is near the net, a good underarm lift can force him or her to turn and try to get back to reach the shuttle. Underarm lifts can be hit on both the forehand and backhand sides.

Holding the racket with a backhand grip, this player lunges forward as he plays a backhand lift shot. He hits the shuttle well in front of him.

This diagram shows the path of the shuttle when hit with different types of shot.

1 Overhead clear
2 Overhead drop shot
3 Smash
4 Defensive clear
5 Attacking clear
6 Net shot

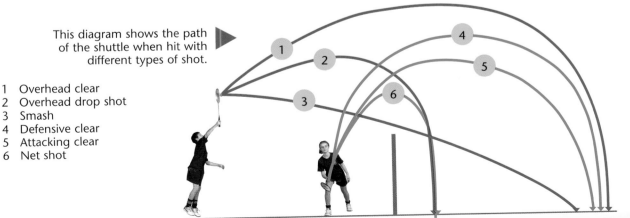

Overhead Clears

The overhead clear shots are played frequently during a game, especially by beginners. They are particularly popular shots in singles where they send the shuttle to the back of the court.

The Forehand Overhead Clear

The forehand clear can be used in two different ways. When under pressure, it can be a defensive shot that sends the shuttle up high into the air. This can buy you the time to get back into a good position. The forehand clear can also be used as an attacking shot when the shot is hit flatter but still clears your opponent's reach on its path to the back of the court.

The Backhand Clear

Whenever possible, try to play a clear shot on your forehand side, because you can generate more power and speed with the

The Forehand Overhead Clear

Elbow pointing upward.

Shuttle hit above and just in front of your head.

1 *Using a forehand grip, get into a good position as the shuttle arrives. With a loose wrist and bent elbow, drop the racket behind your body. Your eyes should follow the shuttle's path.*

2 *Swing the racket up and through the shuttle with a powerful throwing action. Aim to connect with the shuttle at as high a point as possible with your arm fully extended.*

3 *Your racket should follow through forward and finally down. Your body follows with the heel of your back foot lifting off the floor. Then move quickly into a balanced position for your next shot.*

Zhang Ning

Date of Birth: May 19, 1975

Nationality: Chinese

Height: 5ft 9in (1.75m)

Weight: 140lb (64kg)

Achievements

Olympics 2004 Women's Singles gold medal

2003 World Championship Singles winner

2005 and 2006 World Championship Singles runner-up

Tactically strong, with lightning movement, Zhang Ning first played for the Chinese national team at the age of 16. She specializes in singles and won China's first ever Badminton Olympic Gold in 2004. In 2005, Zhang won six major ranking tournaments and reached the final of three more. She continued strongly in 2006, inspiring the Chinese female team to their fifth Uber Cup victory in a row. In the 2008 Olympics she won the gold medal for Women's Singles

Chinese star, Zhang Ning, in action at the 2006 All-England Open Championships. Zhang shows good body position as she plays an overhead clear shot.

forehand than the backhand. Players sometimes use rapid footwork to run around the shuttle's path to turn a backhand shot into a forehand shot. If that is not possible, then a backhand clear shot can be attempted. It sends the shuttle on a similar flight path to the forehand but usually with a little less power.

The Backhand Clear

Racket arm and elbow kept close to body.

Impact point is just behind your head and to your side. Any follow-through that occurs comes from the wrist only.

1 *Using a backhand grip, turn your body so that your back is facing the net. Get your body weight over the foot on the same side as your racket hand. Begin to swing your racket from a low position with your wrist back.*

2 *Aim to hit the shuttle at a high point just behind your head and to your side. Your racket arm should be fully extended, making contact with a strong flick of the wrist. Then turn to face the net.*

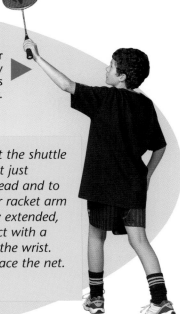

Sidearm Shots

While many shots are played overhead, like the forehand and backhand clears, or underarm, like lifts, there are times when you will need to play shots to your side. The most common sidearm shots are flat drives back down the opponent's sideline, but there are other shots as well.

Drive Shots

Drive shots are often played when the shuttle is to one side but at too low a height to smash. They are particularly common in doubles but are sometimes used in singles as well. Learning to read the flight of the shuttle is important with all badminton shots. With drives, it is important not just to time your shot, but also sometimes to judge whether you need to hit the shot at all—because your opponent's shot may land outside of the court.

The Forehand Drive

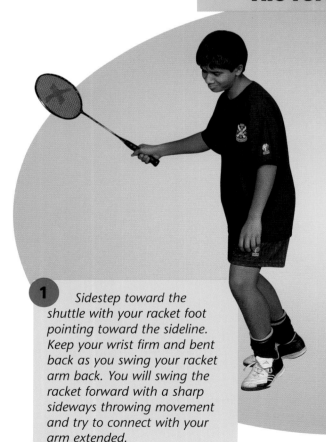

1 *Sidestep toward the shuttle with your racket foot pointing toward the sideline. Keep your wrist firm and bent back as you swing your racket arm back. You will swing the racket forward with a sharp sideways throwing movement and try to connect with your arm extended.*

2 *Swing the racket forward, aiming to hit the shuttle in front of your racket foot. As your racket is about to connect with the shuttle, unbend your wrist. This creates extra power. Your follow-through should first point in the direction of the shot before traveling across your body.*

Drive Variations

There are two important badminton shots that use the basics of the drive but send the shuttlecock on a different path. The cross-court drive sends the shuttle hard, low, and flat across the net to the other side of the court rather than down the sideline. This shot is made by hitting the shuttle a little earlier and more in front of your body, with your racket head angled to send the shuttle across court.

The same basic stance and movement for the drive can also be used to make a sort of sidearm drop shot. This is where the shuttle leaves the racket gently and just drops over the net into your opponent's court. The key is at the very last minute to slow the wrist action and racket swing so that you push the shuttlecock gently rather than hit it hard. Performed well, this can deceive your opponent.

Chinese badminton legend, Gao Ling, hits a forearm drive shot on the way to winning the 2006 All-England Badminton mixed doubles title. She has dramatically slowed her swing at the last moment to turn the drive into a gentle drop shot (see page 25).

The Backhand Drive

1 Step over with your racket leg so that it is nearest the sideline. Adopt the backhand grip and draw your racket back. Keep your elbow high during the backswing and watch the shuttle's flight.

2 As you swing your racket forward, make sure your weight is over your front foot. Hit the shuttle in front of your front foot at the highest point possible. Your wrist, bent back during the backswing, should unbend as impact is made.

21

Net Shots

Playing close to the net is a crucial part of badminton. At different times in a game you will be near the net, playing of the offensive or being forced to defend.

Net Play

Most net shots you play should land near the net on your opponent's side of the court. Always try to hit the shuttle as early and as high as possible. If the shuttle is above net height, you may be able to play an attacking shot. If it is below, aim to play a safe net shot. When playing very close to the net, remember that your racket, any part of your body, and your clothing must not touch the net. Your racket can travel over the net providing it doesn't touch it and the shuttle was hit on your side of the net first.

Net Lunges

Sometimes, you will be on the receiving end of a good net shot. You must always try to return a shot as best as you can. One of the best ways if the shuttle is low is to use a net lunge. Net lunges can be played on both the backhand and forehand side. They involve taking a long step and bending low with your front knee so that you can get your racket underneath the shuttle.

The Backhand Net Lunge

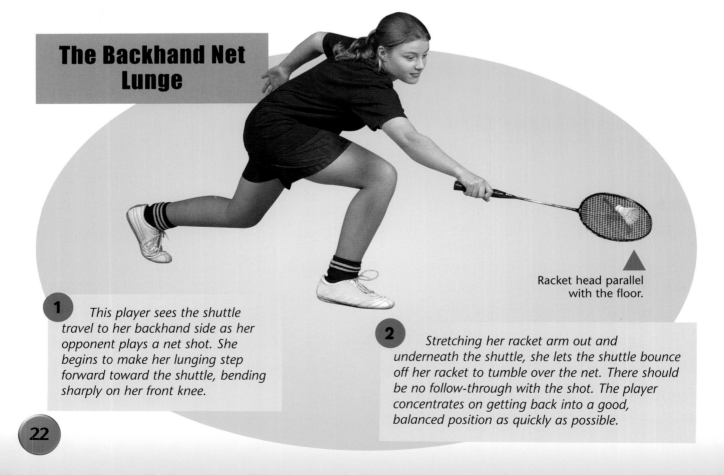

Racket head parallel with the floor.

1 *This player sees the shuttle travel to her backhand side as her opponent plays a net shot. She begins to make her lunging step forward toward the shuttle, bending sharply on her front knee.*

2 *Stretching her racket arm out and underneath the shuttle, she lets the shuttle bounce off her racket to tumble over the net. There should be no follow-through with the shot. The player concentrates on getting back into a good, balanced position as quickly as possible.*

The Net Kill

1 To play a net kill, you must get into position as quickly as possible. Hold your racket high enough to connect with the shuttle above the level of the net. You want to make contact with the shuttle ahead of you.

2 Use your wrist to make the tapping movement of the shot to send the shuttle down and over the net. There should be little or no movement of the rest of your racket arm and no follow-through.

The Net Kill

Sometimes, hitting the shuttle hard at the net allows it to travel higher and farther, which may give your opponent more chance to return it. The net kill is an aggressive shot designed not to give your opponent that chance. It can be used at the net to put away a weak or loose shot. Net kills are played steeply downward with pace into the front of the opponent's court or, occasionally, into the midde of the court.

Olympic Wins

Since badminton's Olympic debut in 1992, players from Asian nations have won 52 of the 61 Olympic medals.

23

Smashes and Drop Shots

Smashes and drop shots are attacking shots which, if performed well, often lead to winning points. They are tricky to master, need to be practiced often, and can only be used in certain situations.

Overhead Smash

The overhead smash is the most powerful shot in badminton. It is often the main weapon of offense in the front and middle of the court. A player will try to work in a rally so that an opponent's weak clear or lift can be pounced on with a smash. Speed is vital to generate power but the position of the racket head in relation to the shuttle is just as vital. Many beginners mistime smashes and hit them too early, with the racket angled too far down, sending the shuttle into the net, or too late, sending the shuttle ballooning up and out of the court.

The Forehand Smash

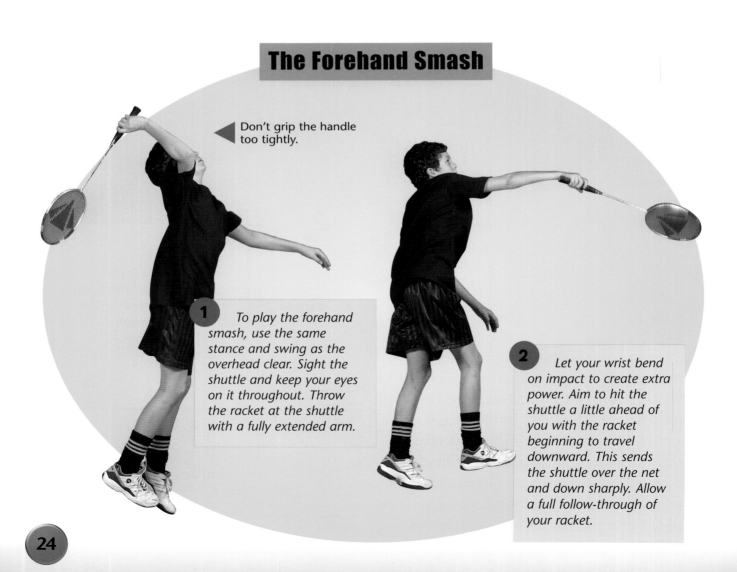

Don't grip the handle too tightly.

1 To play the forehand smash, use the same stance and swing as the overhead clear. Sight the shuttle and keep your eyes on it throughout. Throw the racket at the shuttle with a fully extended arm.

2 Let your wrist bend on impact to create extra power. Aim to hit the shuttle a little ahead of you with the racket beginning to travel downward. This sends the shuttle over the net and down sharply. Allow a full follow-through of your racket.

Top players like Lee Chong Wei jump high to turn a shot heading toward the back of their court into an opportunity to play a powerful overhead smash.

Lee Chong Wei

Date of Birth: October 21, 1982
Nationality: Malaysian

Height: 5ft 8in (1.72m)

Weight: 130lb (60kg)

Achievements

Winner 2006 Asian Badminton Championships

2006 Commonwealth Games gold medal men's singles

2006 Commonwealth Games gold medal team event

2008 Beijing Olympics silver medal men's singles

A rising star of badminton in Malaysia where he wasn't beaten for three years, Chong Wei is light but is fast on the court and has a very strong smash. After a series of tournament wins, in September 2006 he became the world ranked number one male singles player.

This player makes an overhead drop shot, checking his racket's forward movement at impact and trying to stop any follow-through.

Drop Shots

Drop shots are delicate, skillful strokes where it appears you are going to hit the shuttle with medium or maximum force and distance. However, you reduce your swing speed and wrist movement at the very last moment to slow your shot dramatically. The shuttle should gently drop just over the net into your opponent's court.

Overhead drop shots can be played on the forehand or backhand side and have the same movements as an overhead clear. However, just before impact, you check your racket's movement with your wrist bent and aim to follow-through as little as you can. The rest of the shot's movement must be convincing though to deceive your opponent.

Courtcraft

You need more than a wide range of shots to win at badminton. You need to have a sharp brain and good awareness of your opponent and where they are in order to make the most of your shots.

Tactical Tips

There are some handy tactical tips that will apply in many rallies during a match. In general in singles, you should try to get back to a ready position in the center of the midcourt area after making each shot. This position gives you the best chance of reaching your opponent's shots.

Unless you are making a smash straight at the body of your opponent, try to hit the shuttle away from your opponent so that they have to move. Your major aim with all your play is to force your opponent into making a

mistake, so that they hit the shuttle out of bounds or make a weak return that you can latch onto and put away.

There will be many times when you will be on the receiving end of an opponent's attack. When you're struggling out of position, try to buy yourself time to get back into a good position. You can do this by using a high shot, such as a lift to the back of the court.

Strengths and Weaknesses

As you play, pay attention to your opponent's game and abilities so that you can judge their strengths and weaknesses. Many beginners, for example, find it hard to return shots from the back of the court on their backhand side. This is something you can exploit. Try to move your opponent into positions where they have to play their weakest shots and get yourself into positions where you are strongest. But do try to vary your game enough to keep your opponent guessing.

Good awareness of your opponent can help you score points. The player (left) farthest away from us looks to play a simple dab or push shot at the net but seeing her opponent to one side, changes the racket angle to hit the shuttle cross-court and away from her opponent.

This men's doubles pair from Denmark adopt an attacking formation as they serve. The server, Jens Eriksen, stands at the front about to play a low backhand serve while his partner, Martin Lundgaard Hansen is behind him, covering the rear half of the court.

Disguise

Good players win badminton matches often by craftily disguising shots. For example, on the pages 24–25, you saw how the overhead smash and overhead drop shots use much of the same actions as the overhead clear. A good player will try to convince their opponent that they're about to play one of these shots when, in fact, they play another shot.

Doubles and Mixed Doubles

Tactics in doubles badminton have many similarities to singles, as pairs try to play to their strengths and exploit their opponents' weaknesses. Positioning,

Fitness and Footwork

According to a report from Baylor University in Texas, a player will strike the shuttlecock around 400 times during a typical three-game match. A player will also make some 350 major changes of direction during a match. This is why footwork and good stretching before playing is important.

though, is often different to singles and, with two players covering the court per team, pairs have to be really aware of other players' movements. This serving pair in doubles (shown above) have opted for a front and back formation. The server stands at the front and after serving will try to adopt a position in the middle of the front half of the court. Their partner stands behind them and their role is to cover the rear half of the court.

Selected Results

World Men's Singles Champions

Year	Champion	Runner-Up
1980	Rudy Hartono Kurniawan, INA	Liem Swie King, INA
1983	Icuk Sugiarto, INA	Liem Swie King, INA
1985	Han Jian, CHN	Morten Frost, DEN
1987	Yang Yang, CHN	Morten Frost, DEN
1989	Yang Yang, CHN	Ardy Wiranata, INA
1991	Zhao Jianhua, CHN	Allan Budi Kusuma, INA
1993	Joko Suprianto, INA	Hermawan Susanto, INA
1995	Heryanto Arbi, INA	Park Sung Woo, KOR
1997	Peter Rasmussen, DEN	Sun Jun, CHN
1999	Sun Jun, CHN	Fung Permadi, TP
2001	H. Hendrawan, INA	Peter Gade, DEN
2003	Xia Xuanze, CHN	Wong Choong Hann, MAL
2005	Taufik Hidayat, INA	Lin Dan, CHN
2006	Lin Dan, CHN	Bao Chunlai, CHN
2007	Lin Dan, CHN	

World Women's Singles Champions

Year	Champion	Runner-Up
1980	Verawaty Wiharjo INA	Ivana Lie INA
1983	Li Lingwei CHN	Han Aiping CHN
1985	Han Aiping CHN	Wu Jianqui CHN
1987	Han Aiping CHN	Li Lingwei CHN
1989	Li Lingwei CHN	Huang Hua CHN
1991	Tang Jiuhong CHN	Sarwendah Kusumawardhani INA
1993	Susi Susanti INA	Bang Soo Hyun KOR
1995	Ye Zhaoying CHN	Han Jingna CHN
1997	Ye Zhaoying CHN	Gong Zhichao CHN
1999	Camilla Martin DEN	Dai Yun CHN
2001	Gong Ruina CHN	Zhou Mi CHN
2003	Zhang Ning CHN	Gong Ruina CHN
2005	Xie Xingfang CHN	Zhang Ning CHN
2006	Xie Xingfang CHN	Zhang Ning CHN
2007	Zhu Lin, CHN	

The Thomas Cup Men's Team Competition

Year	Champion	Runner-Up
1952	Malaya	United States
1955	Malaya	Denmark
1958	Indonesia	Malaya
1961	Indonesia	Thailand
1964	Indonesia	Denmark
1967	Malaysia	Indonesia
1970	Indonesia	Malaysia
1973	Indonesia	Denmark
1976	Indonesia	Malaysia
1979	Indonesia	Denmark
1982	China	Indonesia
1984	Indonesia	China
1986	China	Indonesia
1988	China	Malaysia
1990	China	Malaysia
1992	Malaysia	Indonesia
1994	Indonesia	Malaysia
1996	Indonesia	Denmark
1998	Indonesia	Malaysia
2000	Indonesia	China
2002	Indonesia	Malaysia
2004	China	Indonesia
2006	China	Denmark
2008	China	Korea

The Uber Cup Women's Team Competition

Year	Champion	Runner-Up
1960	United States	Denmark
1963	United States	England
1966	Japan	United States
1969	Japan	Indonesia
1972	Japan	Indonesia
1975	Indonesia	Japan
1978	Japan	Indonesia
1981	Japan	Indonesia
1984	China	England
1986	China	Indonesia
1988	China	Korea
1990	China	Korea
1992	China	Korea
1994	Indonesia	China
1996	Indonesia	China
1998	China	Indonesia
2000	China	Denmark
2002	China	Korea
2004	China	Korea
2006	China	Netherlands
2008	China	Indonesia

Olympic Medal Table (1992–2008)

Men's Singles, Doubles and Mixed Doubles

Country	Gold	Silver	Bronze	Total
Indonesia	5	5	5	15
Korea	4	6	1	11
China	3	1	2	6
Denmark	1	0	2	3
Malaysia	0	1	2	3
Great Britain	0	1	1	2

Women's Singles and Doubles

Country	Gold	Silver	Bronze	Total
China	6	4	9	19
Korea	2	2	2	6
Indonesia	1	0	0	1
Denmark	0	1	0	1

Glossary

Alley The sideline area between the singles and doubles sidelines.

Back Alley The area between the back boundary line and the long service line for doubles.

Backcourt The back third of the court.

Baseline The back boundary line at each end of the court, parallel to the net.

Center or Base Position Location in the middle of the court to which a singles player tries to return after each shot.

Drop shot A delicate shot in which speed and wrist movement are slowed at the last moment, so that the shuttle drops gently over the net.

Fault A violation of the playing rules, either in serving, receiving, or during play.

Forecourt The front third of the court, between the net and the short service line.

Groin The area where your leg joins your pelvis.

Hamstrings The sinews found in the hollow at the back of the knee.

Midcourt The middle third of the court, halfway between the net and the back boundary line.

Overhead clear A defensive or offensive shot that sends the shuttle to the back of the court.

Quadriceps The front thigh muscles.

Rally The exchange of shots between players while the shuttle is in play.

Serve (Service) The stroke used to put the shuttlecock into play at the start of a rally.

Service court Also called the service box, this is the area into which the serve must be delivered.

Short service line The first line on the court from the net

Smash A powerful overhead shot that sends the shuttle sharply downward.

Websites

www.internationalbadminton.org
Homepage of the Badminton World Federation, the organization responsible for running the world game.

www.worldbadminton.com
A large and very useful collection of links to badminton-based websites, divided up into sections on organizations, clubs, players, equipment and training.

www.usabadminton.org
USA Badminton (USAB) is the recognized national governing body for the sport of badminton in the USA. The USAB oversees all U.S. badminton competitions and prepares the best American players for the Olympic Games. The National Headquarters are located at the U.S. Olympic Training Center in Colorado Springs, Colorado, it is the mission of this nonprofit organization to promote the sport of badminton at all levels across the United States. The website can tell you, region by region, where you can play badminton in the USA. Click on a state to see a listing of where you can play.

www.badmintonengland.co.uk
The homepage of the governing body for the sport in England includes rules, technique tips, and contact details for clubs and competitions.

Note to parents and teachers: every effort has been made by the Publishers to ensure that these websites are suitable for children, that they are of the highest educational value, and that they contain no inappropriate or offensive material. However, because of the nature of the Internet, it is impossible to guarantee that the contents of these sites will not be altered. We strongly advise that Internet access be supervised by a responsible adult.

Index